BLOCKCHAIN

The Evolution of Blockchain: Simple Guide About Blockchain, Bitcoin, and Cryptocurrency

DARRELL FROST

© Copyright 2018 by Darrell Frost - All rights reserved.

The following Book is reproduced below with the goal of providing information that is as accurate and as reliable as possible. Regardless, purchasing this eBook can be seen as consent to the fact that both the publisher and the author of this book are in no way experts on the topics discussed within, and that any recommendations or suggestions made herein are for entertainment purposes only. Professionals should be consulted as needed before undertaking any of the action endorsed herein.

This declaration is deemed fair and valid by both the American Bar Association and the Committee of Publishers Association and is legally binding throughout the United States.

Furthermore, the transmission, duplication or reproduction of any of the following work, including precise information, will be considered an illegal act, irrespective whether it is done electronically or in print. The legality extends to creating a secondary or tertiary copy of the work or a recorded copy and is only allowed with express written consent of the Publisher. All additional rights are reserved.

The information in the following pages is broadly considered to be a truthful and accurate account of facts, and as such any inattention, use or misuse of the information in question by the reader will render any resulting actions solely under their purview. There are no scenarios in which the publisher or the original author of this work can be in any fashion deemed liable for any hardship or damages that may befall them after undertaking information described herein.

Additionally, the information found on the following pages is intended for informational purposes only and should thus be considered, universal. As befitting its nature, the information presented is without assurance regarding its continued validity or interim quality.

Trademarks that mentioned are done without written consent and can in no way be considered an endorsement from the trademark holder

Table of Contents

INTRODUCTION 6

CHAPTER 1: BASIC CONCEPTS OF BLOCKCHAIN 8

DEFINITION OF BLOCKCHAIN 8
THE WORKING OF BLOCKCHAIN 9

CHAPTER 2: MECHANICS OF BLOCKCHAIN 11

USES OF BLOCKCHAIN 11
USERS OF BLOCKCHAIN 17
THE SECURITY OF BLOCKCHAIN 17
THE EXTENSIVENESS OF BLOCKCHAIN 21
THE BLOCKCHAIN'S ROLE IN FUTURE FINANCES 25

CHAPTER 3: THE BLOCKCHAIN FOR YOUR BOTTOM LINE 32

DOES THE BLOCKCHAIN HAVE ANY FLAWS? 35

CHAPTER 4: ROAD TO CRYPTOCURRENCY AND BITCOIN 39

CRYPTOCURRENCIES AND THE BLOCKCHAIN: ENTER TO THE MARKET 39
BITCOIN 42
   Bitcoin Transactions *43*
   Why Bitcoins? *45*
WAYS OF ACQUIRING BITCOINS 45
   Buy On an Exchange *45*
   Transfers *45*
   Mining *46*
WHERE DO YOU STORE BITCOIN? 46
   Types of Wallets *47*
HOW TO SETUP A BITCOIN ACCOUNT 48
HOW DO YOU SEND BITCOIN? 49
BENEFITS OF BITCOIN EXCHANGE 50
   No Taxation *50*
   Flexible Online Payments *50*
   Minimal Transaction Fees *51*

Concealed User Identity *51*
No outside interventions *52*
STRATEGY GUIDE IN CRYPTOCURRENCIES 52
Capitalization of The Market and Volume of Daily Trading *52*
Authentication Method *53*
Approval of Retailers *53*

CHAPTER 5: IMPACT ON WORLD CURRENCY AND OTHER INDUSTRIES 55

BITCOIN AS A VEHICLE FOR INTERNATIONAL TRAVEL 56
Universal *57*
Less costly *57*
Secure *58*
Irreversible *58*
Convenient *58*

CONCLUSION 60

Introduction

Welcome! Let's enter the world of blockchains!

Blockchain technology records financial transactions permanently and updates whenever a new purchase is made. This functional and straightforward description has a significant impact. It allows us to think about old forms that create transactions, store data and move assets.

Block chain's stability is progressing gradually and continues to improve its system on is own. This affects the trust of key institutions (e.g., clearing houses, banks, legislators, governments, and large companies) and allows them to avoid these old checkpoints.

Blockchains are excellent catalysts for change that affect governance, lifestyles, traditional business models, society and international organizations. The subversion of Blockchain is a significant change to all, hence, will find resistance. This also reduces the confidence of key institutions (e.g., banks, legislators, clearing houses, governments, large companies) and allows them to bypass these old checkpoints.

Today, Blockchain pursues a range of services. These include stock trading, online banking, product purchases, order verification and tax filing. However, even if these services are accessible by public databases, there were also other services which verify the blockchains and the authenticity of the information. The transparency of modifications of truth access is expected on the said services.

In this book, you'll learn all the relevant concepts related to blockchain and cryptocurrency. This will include the workings and mechanics of blockchain, its security premises, the Bitcoins and cryptocurrency, the current trend on the blockchain, its impact on the business and other industries as well as its limitations.

Chapter 1: Basic Concepts of Blockchain

Blockchain brings a global revolution as it enters the finance market. Blockchain does not only benefit the industries but the users as well. However, since its introduction to the business market, the visualization is still indistinct. Today, there are still a lot of probes that lingers in everyone's mind.

Definition of Blockchain

For starters, Blockchain allows digital data without risk of consideration. It has, in a certain way, the foundation of a new area of new interior space. Bitcoin was initially developed to encourage people to understand the algorithm functions and hash functions. Nowadays, some of these improvements find other possible uses of this perfect invention that could start a new commercial process in the world.

To define further, Blockchain is a kind of algorithm and data generation framework for the administration of the electronic cash without the mediation of any government or centralized administration. Blockchain, just like other financial workings, also record all the vital information regarding money transactions information and others that also holds value.

The Working of Blockchain

The blockchain is designed to support the Bitcoin cryptocurrency. However, due to many criticisms faced by the system, the technology was alternatively used in other ways. To illustrate what Blockchain is all about, imagine a spreadsheet that records data and networks in a computer system and believe that these are configured from time to time.

Blockchain stores information in which the data is updated in a certain way expected. It is a practical option that has many advantages. This means that it is still to the public for review and confirmation. Moreover, there is no storing platform which can be damaged. It can be easily accessed through some computing systems everywhere, and anyone who has an internet connection can check the data.

Blockchain technology replicates the internet space. The blockchain is the same with the World Wide Web when it comes to sharing of data with the general public.

Blockchain platforms store authentic information and are available to be viewed on various network systems.

However, remember that single person cannot control blockchain, at some time or last and does not have any error. Similar to the internet which has proven itself as a tight space for more the last three decades, Blockchain will also be a reliable and authentic stage for the transaction of industries as it continues to evolve.

Chapter 2: Mechanics of Blockchain

Uses of Blockchain

Think about the Blockchain as an innovation that could empower the "Web of Finances," that you like. We as of now have a financial framework, yet it's a not an efficient one with unnecessary inherent expenses for its clients. Consider it a prepare that loses a great deal of its dynamic vitality to contact and warmth, on the off chance that you like. It could most likely work all the more productively if the track was kept in decent shape and it's intended to run all the more viable on that track. The Blockchain and the system it keeps running on can give the more effective path on the off chance that we can construct the better one.

The Blockchain can be utilized for not just monitoring charges and credits for a money framework like Bitcoin yet in addition to following any information that may include an exchange or record of proprietorship somehow. Estonia is as of now utilizing the Blockchain to tidy up its legal framework. If you have at any point managed a legal official administration somehow, you may have thought about how public accountant specialists realize that their customers aren't conferring pressure.

The genuine truth is that official legal operators can be occupied, tricked or remunerated into empowering extortion and this exact issue is the reason that Estonia collaborated with BitNation to unwind false strategies concerning the legal official open.

An example of the framework that advantages the utilization of Blockchain is the methods for the empowered, smart bolt. This component keeps an occupant to get to the structure as a result of an inability to pay the lease and different contribution on time.

Once you've marked the contract, it's accepted that you knew what you consented to. If you wake up and your carport is void since you missed installments on your auto advance, at any rate, you will know where your auto is. On the other side, the Blockchain secures your rights, as well, via mechanizing the way toward logging installments. You can make your regularly scheduled payments by sending some cryptographic money to a particular address that is checked by the Smart Contract. The auto wouldn't drive itself back to the dealership because the financier neglected to log an installment.

Nobody will imagine that you can get legitimate Ray-Bans for $10. For more immediate things, the Blockchain can monitor where supplies originate. Existing Blockchain inventory network applications incorporate Provenance, which works with organizations to ensure that items extending from fish to knapsacks arise from honest to goodness sources. More noteworthy straightforwardness in the store network is the sort of thing that can gain buyers' trust in this present reality where individuals are ending up progressively mindful of issues, for example, the unlawful or unsustainable reaping of fish on being utilized to deliver items like rucksacks. The Blockchain can give that straightforwardness when used to manufacture a store network application that can ensure the genuineness of items by dismissing any shipment that did not originate from a perceived source.

A work process application can work in a way that is like the store network to bring up places where forms that are critical to your business are getting bottlenecked. Here and there an area or office just isn't being as profitable as it could be. The issue may even be an outsider seller that isn't conveying the quality administration you anticipated. An interior application that adds usefulness to what Trello would already be able to do can take out the observation that you need to endure whatever is causing the bottleneck. With a Blockchain work process application, you get unalterable documentation that you can remain on when you wipe out the reason for the bottleneck.

Notoriety is imperative to business. Organizations will pay cash to outsider audit locales to conceal negative surveys, pay hack journalists to post gleaming audits of their own business or assault a contender with negative reviews or give free items to proficient analysts in return for a "genuine" survey. What a Blockchain notoriety application can accomplish all the more dependable is go about as a sidechain for a Smart Contract application that can read records on the contract chain yet not make new records. This notoriety application can monitor how often that invested individuals have reneged on a contract or activated conditions on their deal that created a discount be issued.

Did an Internet specialist organization throttle the Internet access for its clients? Not exclusively will those clients get a discount from the Smart Contracts included, however, the notoriety sidechain will enroll that as a ding to the ISP's notoriety. Organizations that cooperate to keep up a Smart Contract framework with appended notoriety sidechain can increase upper hand even finished organizations that are individuals from the Business Bureau primarily because it feels less like a straightforward "esteemed gentlemen club" for organizations. Or maybe, it feels like one that is less helpless against "negative survey assault" by a contender since its activity is to monitor the numbers that speak to a business' real execution.

This works because the Blockchain is sufficiently straightforward to make data put away on it simple to hunt and read. It won't influence you to go through the motions, make a record or agree to accept an email pamphlet to get the data you need. If you are searching for data about a Bitcoin installment and have the exchange ID, an IP address or one of the Blockchain tends to engage with the exchange; it's sufficiently pure to look on Blockchain.info for that data.

This sort of straightforwardness can be joined with the way that you aren't putting away your clients' Visa data when they pay with digital currencies to promise them that your mind enough to win their trust. They can type your business name into an inquiry application and find all that they need to think about your business' reputation. It gives the raw numbers in a way that is anything but difficult to peruse. How often have you taken a contract to an effective conclusion? Does the client benefit appear to decrease once you've made the deal, prompting a ton of clients wiping out contracts alone? Likewise, with the work process application, the correct sort of notoriety application can direct you toward the one area or component that may cause issues for generally great business.

So if it requires a reliable and straightforward approach to keep records, the Blockchain can be utilized as a base to construct an application for that. That straightforwardness can promise buyers that the merchant is being straightforward or enable them to maintain a strategic distance from untrustworthy sellers. The Blockchain likewise secures the privileges of the two shoppers and sellers by recording the points of interest of any given exchange, contract or archive on the legal framework in a way that is hard to debate.

Users of Blockchain

There is no defined rule on who can use blockchain. Although these days only banks, huge companies, and global institutions benefit most from this technology. The blockchain is open for the daily business transactions. The only challenge that blockchain faces are the worldwide acceptance.

The Security of Blockchain

The first form of the Blockchain makes utilization of a cryptographic hash known as SHA-256. It's protected however may not be so useful that particular equipment called mining rigs has been made mainly to deal with the activity of preparing exchanges. These mining rigs take care of numerical issues called hashes to affirm and transfer substantial exchanges.

Each explained hash speaks to one piece – a heap of handled exchanges that can be handed-off to every single substantial hub. The cryptographic data contains a unique timestamp, which makes perceptions of the Blockchain look like connections in a chain.

This chain of squares makes it simple to distinguish endeavors to add records to the chain deceitfully. Envision that you're adding connections to a chain and somebody tags along, picks a relationship amidst the chain and begins adding a person's own connects to that connection. The chain has recently been forked. That defective refresh can also fork the Blockchain in 2013. However, the quick response by Bitcoin designers demonstrates that it's conceivable to perceive and seclude a deceitful fork if it happens rapidly.

For what reason would someone deceitfully fork a Blockchain? They may do it since they need to alter a record that as of now exists on the chain erroneously, so they fork the chain just before the piece that contains that record. This may turn into a typical strategy with any individual who wishes to deceitfully modify a contract, deed or title if endeavors to fork the chain are not identified and blue-penciled too rapidly to make such an attempt worth the exertion and hazard.

They may fork a Blockchain because they wish to take control of the framework through and through. Of course, the rendition of the chain that can order all the more preparing force and, along these lines, make the most extended chain of pieces is viewed as the legitimate one.

Bitcoin frequently sets world records with the measure of handling power it summons so that the vast majority would view an assault on Bitcoin as costlier than its value, yet most Blockchain organizes merely don't charge that much preparing power. Some individual who needs to assume control over a relinquished digital money wouldn't need to fork it by any stretch of the imagination. He could just set up a hub or two and a couple of humble mining apparatuses to take a shot at approving new records as a feature of the way toward rebooting it.

In the two cases, it's sufficiently straightforward to analyze the cryptographic hash and timestamp of the records being referred to figure out which is the first, legitimate record. The incidental 2013 division was settled by notice excavators to not change over to the "new" rendition of the Bitcoin Blockchain. Even though the Blockchain is intended to be secure, this additionally exhibits the benefit of having ready specialists and engineers on the scene on the off chance that a fork happens.

An alarm Blockchain master can seclude a hub that is breaking down or hinting at altering and explore the issue. Possibly the center is regurgitating phony and counter-intuitive records. Perhaps the center isn't handing-off new records by any means. Maybe the center has made its particular little form of the Blockchain, and that is the point at which the Blockchain master is hugely going to begin asking the serious inquiries. Why is it forked, and what sort of silliness is the branch chief associated with now?

This is indeed one of the gains of having a decentralized framework that can deal with various hubs more than one area. It's anything but confusing to seclude a "maverick" center for investigating without bargaining whatever remains of the framework. The carrying on hubs can merely continue stopping without end, making new legitimate records and making them accessible for any individual who needs to review or utilize them, while the Blockchain master examines what turned out badly with the getting out of hand hub.

The Extensiveness of Blockchain

Present-day Western culture thinks about including whatever number individuals as could be expected under the circumstances in its financial framework, yet the integrated commercial structure hasn't gotten the update yet.

Two billion people don't have convenient or modest access to managing account administrations. What makes the Blockchain diverse is that it can be as comprehensive as you can imagine.

It doesn't make a difference to the Blockchain on the off chance that you have no benefits and no personal ID card to appear. The Bitcoin wallet is a customer that associates with hubs on the Bitcoin organize. Bitcoin is more comprehensive than banks since you don't need to build up quite a bit of anything except for your capacity to utilize that customer. That is something that should make digital forms of money prominent with the destitute who don't have a road address, however, do have a shoddy PC that works.

To the Blockchain, decency is the capacity to utilize its framework on an equal balance with each other client. If you are a freelancer, you may offer on employment on destinations like XBTFreelancer alongside each other freelancer who is occupied with making a Bitcoin. If you have some utilized things that you need to provide yet would prefer not to use eBay, you may attempt Bitify. You may even have some fortunes with purchasing and delivering on the Bitcointalk Marketplace if you can endure establishing yourself as a significant aspect of the Bitcoin people group first. The point here is that Blockchain applications like Bitcoin are astoundingly simple to begin utilizing close to downloading the customer regardless of your identity.

This is genuine even in nations where Paypal doesn't work, and the utilization of charge cards isn't ordinary. Numerous members of a few nations' commercial centers like to utilize money or what might as well be called money since it's merely more helpful than heading off to the bank.

Kenya's MPesa is a win for precisely this reason. Because the business visionary is thinking about growing activities into one of these nations or even merely enlisting the intermittent freelancer who dwells in a zone where Paypal won't work, this is something that should be represented. From the viewpoint of somebody living in one of these nations, on the off chance that he can't pay or be paid with cash like MPesa or Bitcoin or a couple of paper charges in his local money, he's not going to see the utilization of taking an interest. So utilizing Bitcoin and the Blockchain can without much of a stretch help you, as a business visionary, take an interest in the overall market.

Regardless of whether you lean toward not to make your character known (and no one at any point did dependably affirm Bitcoin maker Satoshi Nakamoto's genuine personality), Bitcoin makes it conceivable to work together anyplace whenever. Bitcoin crosses universal outskirts effectively, which makes it progressively prevalent for Filipinos working abroad who need to send cash to their families in the Philippines. In its unadulterated shape, Bitcoin is shabby, quick, secure, and will get your cash under the control of the beneficiaries while seldom, if at any point, being contacted by outsiders who will need their cut of the pie.

The Blockchain can do a similar thing since, well, it was presented as a feature of the Bitcoin bundle. Bitcoin betting locales utilize the expression "provably reasonable" to demonstrate that their calculations have not been unjustifiably weighted against its players notwithstanding when the chances are now against them. Dice amusements are sufficiently hard to win notwithstanding when the dice aren't stacked. Substances that are keen on utilizing the Blockchain ought to receive the idea of "provably reasonable" to guarantee that everyone can take an interest in voluntary exchanges without the deck being stacked in the house's support notwithstanding when they begin with nothing and the chances are as of now against them.

This implies there ought to be no manufactured boundaries to get. There ought to be no section expenses (past getting a cell phone that is fit for running your preferred Blockchain customer), and a well-disposed condition for organizations who will go out on a limb engaged with executing with individuals they may never know the names. I can purchase a pizza with a couple of hundredths of a Bitcoin, and they never need to record my name or financial data in any changeless shape.

The Blockchain's Role in Future Finances

Most business people don't ponder what the monetary atmosphere will look like hundreds of years from now. They're contemplating how their business can get past the following month, quarter, and year. In any case, exceptionally active business people ordinarily have a long haul arrange for that will get them through the coming ten years. The quarterly report matters however so do ensure the business will at present be significant when purchasers proceed onward to the following enormous thing.

Consequently, it pays to actualize the apparatuses that an adroit business person needs to remain adaptable. Purchasers are winding up progressively worried about where the items they purchase each day originate from, so a Blockchain inventory network application can promise them that the things you offer arise from reliable and maintainable sources alongside empowering you to keep away from misrepresentation anytime in the production network. An inside work process application can give you a reasonable picture of how smoothly activities are continuing inside your business and respond all the more rapidly to places where the work process is getting bottlenecked. As essentially for your business, the Blockchain can empower you to contend on a universal playing field by making it conceivable to draw in worldwide clients with a diminished dependence on global outsider budgetary establishments.

Now, the Blockchain could be known as a temporary fad. However, it's not one that is crazy and will crash. The customarily utilized offering focuses utilized by Bitcoin supporters are that it's shoddy, quick, secure, and ensures the privileges of the beneficiary. When you complete a considerable measure of universal business, the Bitcoin that global clients send to you will, for the most part, be in your wallet in 60 minutes, tops. When you send cash to a worldwide contractor, he'll like that he doesn't need to hold up days to get his cash as he would if you utilize Western Union or PayPal. Bitcoin will even work in countries that PayPal doesn't, so you'll never at any point need to think about whether your contractor got his cash as long as you sent it to the privilege Bitcoin address. Blockchain applications can utilize similar properties that make it simple for Bitcoin to jump over worldwide fringes to ensure the interests of all gatherings in an exchange paying little heed to where they are on the planet.

This makes the Blockchain valuable for an economy that is progressively worldwide. For instance, you're a US resident; you could go without much of a stretch contract a French consultant to decipher some content from American English to French to use on the French-dialect adaptation of your site. He may demand being paid in X measure of Bitcoin just because it's less demanding than agonizing over cash trade rates. That same consultant could then utilize that Bitcoin to pay for his costs regardless of whether he doesn't have a financial balance. He can genuinely use Bitcoin to purchase a pizza, and the pizza put doesn't have to know his name, considerably less his budgetary data.

This conveys us to the following fascinating point about what the Blockchain could empower for the eventual fate of financial matters. Global associations have assessed that upwards of two billion individuals can't advantageously get to the money related administrations that whatever remains of us underestimate. They may need to stroll for two days to get to a bank. They won't have the capacity to open a financial balance. Banks may charge high expenses for the "comfort" of getting the money for a paycheck if the holder of that check does not have a record. The vast majority of these individuals abandon purchasing and offering on an equal balance with whatever remains of us mostly because the banks treat them unreasonably.

Notwithstanding, Blockchain applications and digital forms of money like Bitcoin can incorporate these individuals. Not at all like banks, Bitcoin does not give it a second thought on the off chance that you have no advantages. A Blockchain Smart Contract application would say a remark impact of, "Sign here and keep in mind to make your installments or turn in your work on time," without requiring verification of character. Similar hands that weave a bin can likewise log that container on a Blockchain store network application utilized by retailers that offer Fair Trade items.

At the point when a national monetary framework incorporates more workers that can offer their work on the open market at a sound cost, one of the primary things that country sees are a sharp increment in its GDP. This happens because more individuals are purchasing and offering on an equal balance.

That country may have seen an ongoing convergence of legitimate and persevering workers, or it might have as of late had an active social equality battle that persuaded the neighborhood world class of the benefit of incorporating beforehand minimized gatherings in its standard financial framework.

An expansion in populace alone does not generally measure up to any considerable bounce in esteem delivered per capita, yet an extension of a region's populace that is currently purchasing and offering products and enterprises on the open market does.

The same can be valid in a Blockchain-based fiscal framework in which no one needs to demonstrate a legitimate personal ID card or have the capacity to confirm a PayPal account with a definite end goal to purchase and offer on the universal market. At the point when these two billion unbanked individuals approach cryptographic money and Blockchain customers, you can procure them to deal with those undertakings that aren't generally worth enlisting a lasting representative for however should be done at any rate, and they can utilize those digital currencies to purchase the merchandise and enterprises they require. This involves down to earth financial aspects and not merely axioms. At the point when more individuals are incorporated into an economic framework and can purchase and offer in a genuinely free market, it enhances everyone because it delivers more esteem per capita.

This issues for a similar reason that expert football players once in a while grumble notwithstanding when they lose on the off chance that they realize that the playing field was level, the balls weren't flattened by a con artist on the other group, and the refs did not support one group over the other. A genuinely free market that incorporates advancements like the Blockchain sets things up with the goal that no unified expert can pick champs and washouts. It just ensures everyone gets an opportunity to play.

Hence, the Blockchain could be known as a genuinely 21st-century money related innovation that can understand the wasteful aspects of a comprehensive budgetary framework that hasn't gotten the reminder yet. The possibility of a financial future that incorporates decentralized FinTech is beneficial for you as an entrepreneur who perhaps isn't prepared to contend on the global market, however, wouldn't see any problems with employing a worldwide consultant to deal with an irregular occupation from time to time. That is additionally useful for the unbanked who might genuinely have a remark if no one but they could take an interest in the overall commercial center on an all the more notwithstanding balance. That is the sort of financial future the Blockchain could empower.

Chapter 3: The Blockchain for Your Bottom Line

The main issue here is that the Blockchain is useful for your primary concern on the off chance that you think about remaining sufficiently adaptable to stay applicable. As we've seen with current fashions like Beanie Babies and Pokemon, these things can go back and forth before you can even squint and you need to make utilization of advancements that make them stay control notwithstanding when the present successes can turn into the following day's complimentary gifts. The Blockchain could have that fortitude among worldwide organizations basically because it can make money related dealings considerably more productive without agonizing over what the outside trade will do in particular. It's expected that a Bitcoin is a Bitcoin paying little mind to whether you spend it in the U.S., France, or Japan.

With Blockchain innovation, you can send cash to or get cash from anyplace on the planet economically and rapidly. You can shape contracts with anybody, anyplace, whenever, with not very many stresses over whether the other party is going really to finish.

You can rapidly examine the notoriety of any gathering you're thinking about working with, find any issues with your inventory network, and check the legal framework to see who right now claims a benefit. You can do this with not very many stresses over an outsider getting into the center of exchange and denying you consent to utilize what you possess.

The Blockchain can deal with this since it's intended to store information in a straightforward, idiot proof and cryptographically secure way. Bitcoin and Blockchain insiders jump at the chance to utilize the expression "trustless" to depict you, in fact, don't host to believe the third get-together to use the innovation. On the off chance that you have the decision between taking a risk on an outsider merchant and putting on a show of being a controlled crack who demands that everything is done in-house, be a controlled crack. That way, your clients realize that you think about controlling whatever number factors as could reasonably be expected when they believe you with their data.

It may sound impossible to miss that utilizing trustless innovation along these lines can prompt more noteworthy trust from your clients. Nonetheless, if an outsider merchant you trusted to store information is observed to disregard information security controls, you will typically be discovered at risk for fines and conceivable pay of clients for money related misfortunes they endured because you picked the wrong seller. The contention that an outsider merchant fizzled you is probably not going to awe your clients or a jury. Along these lines, you can contact a specialist who can set up your Blockchain applications and introduce hubs at every one of your areas for you.

The coolest part? You can utilize Bitcoin to pay for part of your costs of doing business rather than dumping it on the trades. Gyft and eGifter both offer electronic gift vouchers that can be utilized to purchase office supplies, pay for your next business trip, get the tab at a supper meeting, or complete a giveaway as a significant aspect of a modest online networking advancement. Next time you procure a specialist or contractor, inquire as to whether they acknowledge Bitcoin.

Nowadays, it's undeniably likely that they'll say yes and send you their Bitcoin address, mostly because they think about not holding up days to get their cash after the activity is done because Western Union and Paypal are taking as much time as is needed. That is something to be thankful for you, particularly on the off chance that you can get the specialist or contractor to sign a Smart Contract as a significant aspect of the procedure carefully. At that point liquidating out moves toward becoming another person's concern while you utilize the Blockchain to keep your business running efficiently.

Does The Blockchain Have Any Flaws?

The straightforward response to this is not a lot of if you actualize the Blockchain as a component of a general Information Technology system. The Blockchain is an almost idiot proof approach to process and store information, however, might be vulnerable to fake performing artists running phony hubs, for example, Chainalysis did in 2015 in what was known as an incomplete Sybil assault. It was found running phony centers that customers could associate. However, these hubs were not transferring information to different centers on the Bitcoin arrange. This is one of a couple of security worries that clients of Blockchain applications should keep an eye out.

This implies having an approach to confirm that the hubs interfacing with your system is legitimate ones that are transmitting substantial information and that the customers associating with them are valid, also. While Bitcoin clients are acclimated with the possibility that anybody with a modest Android tablet can download a wallet, entrepreneurs will lean toward an approach to guarantee that lone approved workers and gadgets can make new records. Your IT staff might have the capacity to cooperate with Blockchain engineers to create a "Blockchain Active Directory" that oversees get to benefits for the two representatives and clients.

For the individuals who are not exceptionally comfortable with Active Directory, it works by sorting out clients into gatherings and after that appointing access benefits to specific assets to each group. The bookkeeping office may approach the month to month cost reports, yet not the agreements with clients. Administrators may contact investigations of the work process information so they can bind bottlenecks. Clients may be able to see their contracts, get refreshes on the status of any requests they've put, and demand updates to their data through a particular customer when proper. So Active Directory ordinarily works by arranging access to assets by work.

It may even be a wise decision to use semi-free sidechains for each capacity. Not very many Blockchain specialists will suggest utilizing only one Blockchain for all your vital information since then you're risking Blockchain swell. This implies a Blockchain can require more stockpiling limit and more preparing power than it ultimately needs to because it's attempting to store excessively information. This turns into a worry when you don't wish to save your bookkeeping records, contracts and work process sign in a similar database.

Instead, Blockchain designers will suggest utilizing separate Blockchains that are frequently called sidechains because they can run parallel to each other, collaborating just as important to serve their capacities. This can accelerate the way toward making new records and seeking through existing files, and improve the approach toward dealing with the Bitcoin Active Directory.

On the off chance that shielding touchy information from being stolen is a worry, you may dither to execute an innovation that guarantees add up to straightforwardness to any individual who is occupied with assessing records. From one viewpoint, such straightforwardness can give you an upper hand with keen shoppers who think about working with somebody who is dependable and utilizes capable sourcing rehearses. On the other, a contender may take information from your R&D division and use that data to patent a conceivable future item before you can. That implies dealing with the Blockchain's straightforwardness admirably.

There are just a predetermined number of approaches to counter the Blockchain's straightforward nature but to execute a vigorous IT security convention for servers on which the Blockchain applications are put away. Nonetheless, Blockchains can be set up, so they don't interface with each other at all and won't realize that another Blockchain exists. The applications can be actualized in a way that enables them to peruse information on a chain however not compose information to that chain, and it's even feasible for one Blockchain record to send "exchanges" to another Blockchain record yet not get "exchanges" from that other record consequently.

Chapter 4: Road to Cryptocurrency and Bitcoin

Cryptocurrencies and The Blockchain: Enter to The Market

Do you recall the Bitcoin Bowl? I won't be exceptionally astounded on the off chance that you don't. BitPay supported the St. Petersburg Bowl for one year, yet then hauled out because it wasn't as effective as BitPay had trusted. If anything, it gave football fans who went to the St. Petersburg Bowl an opportunity to utilize Bitcoin to pay for concessions and trinkets at the stadium.

Be that as it may, business people can utilize cryptographic forms of money and the Blockchain as a more fruitful approach to showcase their organizations. Introduce a Bitcoin ATM and run an advancement. "Triple focuses on your prizes card if you purchase with Bitcoin!" Hand out a reality sheet clarifying what Bitcoin is. At the point when clients become acclimated to paying for their buys utilizing this new Internet cash that so as of late bested $600 in esteem, that is the point at which you can begin presenting the idea of using Blockchain applications as a component of the ordinary business.

Instruction is imperative here. Now, they most likely couldn't care less what sort of record you use as long as you aren't fudging the numbers excessively. Notwithstanding, they do mind that they won't be charged an early cancelation expense at a participation rec center because an unscrupulous director changed the marking date on their contract. It has been known to happen, and clients are exceptionally delicate about extortion on that level. They have to realize that your business and its representatives are never going to be allowed to stoop that low. They get a kick out of the chance to understand that they can believe you regardless of what sort of business you run. So teaching them about what the Blockchain can improve the situation them can turn into a compelling piece of a showcasing drive.

You may have seen those recordings that were fundamentally a prologue to Bitcoin 101. They can clarify Bitcoin in plain English to individuals who've never known about it, aside from possibly in the daily papers, and they believe it's this Internet cash that appears to run as one with the Dark Web. You can demonstrate them generally by running your arrangement of recordings that clarifies that not exclusively can Bitcoin and the Blockchain be utilized for honest to goodness purposes, yet they can likewise be used to guarantee that clients are managing legitimate and straightforward organizations like yours.

"On the off chance that our Internet benefit ever dips under the speed that we ensured, our Blockchain-based contract administration framework will naturally issue a credit on your bill or give you a discount."

"We track our wellsprings of fish on a straightforward Blockchain inventory network framework with the goal that you can see where your fish buys are originating from."

This is the sort of thing that can snare clients that will be around for the whole deal. The gecko is charming, however, "15 minutes can spare you 15% on your auto protection" is the thing that inspires individuals to look at the Geico site. It's data that the client can utilize wrapped up in an organization that is anything but challenging to recollect notwithstanding when the client doesn't make a move immediately. On the off chance that you can accomplish something comparable for the Blockchain, it tells individuals that you're utilizing another sort of innovation that can profit them as much as it benefits you.

Clients are brilliant nowadays. They don't fall for the jingle. Instead, they need to comprehend what makes you not entirely the same as the more significant part of your rivals. That is the reason you should work the Blockchain applications you choose to use into your advertising effort.

Bitcoin

Bitcoin is known as the first decentralized currency. They can be sent conveniently through the Internet. Bitcoin started last 2009. The creator's name is unknown, but the name Nakamoto was coined to this person or group.

Soon after, there is a new type of money for the internet that works in the area of real currency. Bitcoin initializes the peer-to-peer test payment for people without authority; a new currency concept that was introduced in 1998. Cryptography allows the creation and dissemination of money. Because it is the second system and there is no centralized solution, its users around the world manage and control it equally.

Bitcoin Transactions

Bitcoin transactions are created precisely from person to another using the internet. There is no need for a bank or a clearing house to have the opportunity. Thanks to these, the fees for Bitcoin transactions are much lower; they can be used in different countries worldwide. Bitcoin accounts cannot be frozen, and the conditions for not opening it do not exist. Recently, more merchants begin to accept this type of transactions. You can easily purchase anything you want through the use of Bitcoins.

You can work with the exchange, but it works with any other type of trade. As with transactions, Bitcoin Exchange makes it happen quickly. In a manner analogous to physical trading, the buyer has to purchase Bitcoins. The difference is that the person has to register an account in Bitcoin Exchanger. From that, the payment asset of the user will now be in the digital currency form that can be used to buy products. The difference with the others will be there in the way of precisely what can be used to risk any price. Moreover, you can also exchange Bitcoins for other Bitcoins. The process is the same with transferring money that happens in the banks.

In almost all payment methods, the payments are reversed after making Paypal or credit card transactions. However, the situation is different with Bitcoin as once a purchase is created; you can no longer modify it. To avoid facing chargeback problems, be extra careful when exchanging Bitcoins with the currency. It is advisable to do Bitcoin exchanges with other Bitcoin holders near you.

Exchanging dollars, euros, and others to Bitcoin is possible. Purchasing and selling through Bitcoin is not a problem as it was the same as another country's currency. In this case, wallets are needed to store and keep your Bitcoins. Wallets are located on your desktop, mobile devices, and other third-party websites. Sending Bitcoins is as simple as sending an email. Practically speaking, you can purchase anything with Bitcoins.

Moreover, making a Bitcoin transaction does not require you to provide your identity. Every Bitcoin transaction made is recorded to what we call the public log. The general log contains wallet IDs and not people's real names. With that said, the transaction is still private, and you don't have to worry to be tracked when purchasing or selling items.

Why Bitcoins?

As said, Bitcoins do not require your identity to purchase any items. You can appear anonymously. With Bitcoins, payments are relatively easy and cheap since Bitcoins are not under by any country. They are not knotted to any policies. Small enterprises love Bitcoins as there are no credit card fees included. Some purchase Bitcoins for investment purposes and expect these to raise its value for an extended period.

Ways of Acquiring Bitcoins

Buy On an Exchange

Bitcoin exchanges are where people can buy or sell Bitcoins. They do this by using whatever currencies they have.

Transfers

Doing Bitcoin transfers is easy. They can do this by using their mobile phones, PCs or by website platforms. Bitcoin transfers are similar to sending cash digitally.

Mining

Miners secure the Bitcoin network. Above all, they are relevant to all observed transactions. These transactions are entirely audited and then recorded in a transparent public ledger. These individuals contend in mining Bitcoins with use of computer hardware in solving complex mathematical problems. Miners invest in computer hardware. Today, most miners make use of cloud mining. In cloud mining, miners can spend money in third party websites which possess the required infrastructure and reduce costs in usage and energy consumption

Where Do You Store Bitcoin?

The digital wallet is where Bitcoins are stored; it exists in the person's computers and cloud. The digital wallet is the same as a virtual bank account. It allows people to send and receive Bitcoins, purchase items or directly save it. However, the only difference between Bitcoin wallets and bank accounts is that it is not FDIC insured.

Types of Wallets

Online Bitcoin Wallets

Online Bitcoin wallets can be opened and retrieved on the web by any internet devices.

Desktop Wallet

A desktop wallet provides more security than the online wallet as it can only be accessed through your personal computer with your secret passcode in it. Since online wallets are accessible by any internet connected devices, it has a high vulnerability to probable hacking. With that, a security breach is diminished. On the other hand, desktop wallets are not exempted for possible hacks if your computer is infected by a virus that aims to unlock the passcode and steal Bitcoins.

Wallet In The Cloud

One of the advantages of wallet in the cloud is that there is no need for software installation and wait for they synching systems. Just like with the other wallets, even if the security is heightened, hacking is entirely possible too, and the person might lose their Bitcoins.

Hardware Wallet

A hardware wallet is safer than a desktop wallet. Samples of hardware wallets include USB drives which you can bring with you anywhere you go. Hardware wallets also able you to transact anonymously. There is no need to put personal information here, so identity leakage is not to worry.

Paper Wallet

Another relatively safe way to store Bitcoin is to use a paper wallet. However, before getting one, you need to understand better how digital currencies work. To create a paper wallet, you will need to utilize different reliable websites or generate the wallet offline to make it more secure. Paper wallets don't consume much space and also secures your data anonymously, hence, storing Bitcoins is easy on this one.

How to Setup a Bitcoin Account

The blockchain is a Bitcoin broker where you can acquire your Bitcoin wallet. Upon opening a wallet from a certified broker, a Bitcoin address will be given to you which includes a series of letters and numbers the same with your bank account number. A passcode is also provided which will serve as a private key to your Bitcoin wallet.

How Do You Send Bitcoin?

To send bitcoins as a payment for the items and services you want to have, you need to have your Bitcoin address, your passcode, and the receiver's Bitcoin address. All this information is required in your Bitcoin wallet to send some Bitcoins to other Bitcoin holders.

Benefits of Bitcoin Exchange

No Taxation

Commonly, additional money is sent to the government in the form of tax when you make payments using dollars, euros and other currencies. Each item has its specific tax rate. On the other hand, when you use Bitcoin in purchasing, no taxes are added to your order slip. Most Bitcoin users take this chance to buy luxurious items available abroad. Zero tax does not mean it is not an illegal form of tax evasion, hence one of the benefits of being a Bitcoin user.

Flexible Online Payments

Just like any other system, Bitcoin is an online payment system that allows users to pay their coins to purchase luxury items from different parts of the world. Once your Bitcoin wallet is generated and you have an internet connection, you can lie on your bed and purchase coins instead of going to the bank, withdraw your money and go to the store to buy the things that you need.

Also, Bitcoin online payment requires no personal information. Transactions in Bitcoins are a lot easier and more straightforward than those that carry out debit and credit cards.

Minimal Transaction Fees

Extra fees and exchange costs are added on international purchases and wire transfers as a part of regular dues and charges. However, when it comes to Bitcoin, no middle institution or government agency monitors or moderates the charges. With that, transaction costs are kept very low as opposed to the transactions made through the traditional currencies.

Moreover, Bitcoin transactions are not time-consuming because it does not require authorization and waiting for approval phases.

Concealed User Identity

Transacting through bitcoins is discrete because it provides anonymous identity. Bitcoins allow you to purchase items without tracking your transactions made and link to your status. In fact, Bitcoin address never repeats on the same or two different Bitcoin transactions unless you try the option of revealing your purchases. However, in most instances, users tend to keep their identities unpublished.

No outside interventions

Bitcoin transactions disregard outside party interruptions. This means that there are no authorities like banks, financial agencies, or governments that can interrupt the user transactions or freeze a Bitcoin account. As stated, Bitcoin is based on a peer-to-peer system meaning; Bitcoin users can enjoy the freedom of making Bitcoin purchasing than on the conventional purchasing of using the common currencies.

Strategy Guide in Cryptocurrencies

Cryptocurrencies utilizes unique algorithms and is traded in various ways. In this part, you will see the main characteristics of cryptocurrencies that will help you to pick the best cryptocurrency to invest.

Capitalization of The Market and Volume of Daily Trading

The capitalization in the market of cryptocurrency is the sum of all the coins circulating on the present time. A good mark or high value of a currency is determined by the high accessibility of the money in the market and high showcase capitalization. Daily trading is given with more relevance than the volume of the market capitalization: the average of exchanged currencies per day. There is a significance between the high amount of daily trading and top showcase market capitalization in the indication of stable economy of various transactions.

Authentication Method

Authentication is one of the requirements in cryptocurrencies. The most established and commonly used in authenticating is the proof of work. However, the problematic part of this method is that it needs a vast amount of energy to function. Clients with the highest amount of share are allowed to confirm their transactions made. This structure helps to speed up the trading process. On the other hand, due to security concerns of the framework, only a few coins can be utilized.

Approval of Retailers

Cryptocurrency has no essence if you cannot purchase anything with it. So before investing in it, it is essential to know who accepts it. In fact, only a few cryptocurrencies are widely accepted. Since there is a limited acceptance, only few can be traded for other cryptocurrencies. There are coins which cannot merely exchange for items and are only useful for other purposes.

In the world of finance, cryptocurrencies are in an exciting phase. The direction of technology is still unknown but ensures that these new currencies will provide benefits and possibilities that the current cash cannot.

Chapter 5: Impact on World Currency and Other Industries

According to a research, it is expected that there will be five million active Bitcoin users by 2019. For now, the hot debate of cryptocurrency's potential to enter the world of currency and technology continues.

Unlike the traditional banking, Bitcoin currency enables second and immediate only payments without having to go through the complicated process of channeling money. One of the issues the Bitcoin currency is facing its worldwide acceptance. The reason for this is the question of its safety and stability as no government mediates in it, unlike the conventional money banking. What happens is that Bitcoin regulates on its own and allows miners to produce the new coins at the pace. Though the design of creating coins is complicated, it is still advantageous to achieve a steady stream of coins' production.

More companies have been using Bitcoins, and those that adopt this are Microsoft, Tesla, and Dell. Bitcoin transactions are not only for bigger companies, but some companies also make use of Bitcoins that allow you to buy food, beverages, and flowers.

The Bitcoin currency is continually expanding its growth and gradually being accepted by some retailers as they become aware of this. With its increasing acceptance, you too should be confident in Bitcoin. Some obstacles prevent Bitcoin currency for being mainstream. Last March 2017, Bitcoin Exchange Trading Fund sent their initial proposal but was turned down by the US regulators. This could have been a stepping stone for Bitcoin in the aspect of exchanges but what they see is that their currency price goes down. Because of the rejection of large institutions, it is now quite tricky how Bitcoin can become a widely accepted and utilized currency. However, Bitcoin continues to make further attempts to get their desired list. In time, they hope that their persistence will determine the Bitcoin's success.

Bitcoin as A Vehicle for International Travel

The Bitcoin phenomenon enters the financial world due to the attempt of acquiring convenience of people at the top. It was invested so that people can deal with their money and purchases efficiently and no hassle. Bitcoin is a virtual currency that replaced the small traditional bank checks. Some banks and industries are studying the works of

Bitcoin and engage their customers to take it up as a mode of payment because it is smooth and not time-consuming. To track your previous transactions and currency exchange rates, you can check it on a Bitcoin chart. In this chapter, I will discuss you Bitcoin should be on your must-to-have list:

Universal

When you are traveling, the process of exchanging currency is quite cumbersome. The problem gets worse when you go from one place to the other. Also, carrying a considerable amount of cash puts you at risk. Bitcoins give you the comfort of carrying as much money as you need a virtual state. Bitcoins help the traders worldwide by offering convenience on dealing money with more than one currency.

Less costly

When you trade using cash, you are subject to abrupt price changes in essential commodities. You end up spending much more than you had budgeted because of punitive exchange rates. Bitcoins are a global currency that has stable rates and value and will save you the time and high fees.

Secure

Bitcoins are fraud proof due to the heavy cryptography that goes into its making. There are no incidences of hacking or leaking of people's personal information. When you use the conventional money transfer methods abroad, you are likely to fall into the hands of hackers who might infiltrate your bank accounts. With Bitcoin, you alone have access to your account and can authorize any money into and from it.

Irreversible

As a seller, you have probably experienced a situation where a client reverses an already complete transaction. Bitcoin protects you from such incidences, as these transfers cannot be reversed. You should be careful with your Bitcoins, however, as to avoid transferring them to the wrong person.

Convenient

Unlike normal banks that require proof of identification to open an account, Bitcoins allow anyone to access it without asking for proof. Transactions are instant and are not limited by geographical boundaries or time zones, and there is no paperwork involved. To trade Bitcoins, you only need to download the Bitcoin wallet and create an account. You will also never be turned away from opening a Bitcoin account if you are on Chex Systems or owe money to a financial institution.

Conclusion

"Is Blockchain ideal for you?"

Bitcoin is somewhat challenging to decimate. Incapacitating its system would require to turn down the whole World Wide Web, and, after it's all said and done, there might even now be a useful hub in a shelter someplace. Setting up your particular Blockchain framework can be as simple as facilitating it on a server in your storm cellar if your business isn't yet at the point where you have various areas. On the off chance that you can set up more than one server in different areas, this has the impact of robotizing the formation of reinforcements progressively and accelerating the way toward recuperating from a glitch in one of the servers.

In any case, this ought not to be utilized as a reason for overlooking the way that clients believe you with your charge card data. The genuine truth is that being an independent company ought not to be utilized as a reason for disregarding security. Directions in regards to the capacity of MasterCard data apply to you as much as it pertains to huge retailers like Target – who, to the extent, programmers were concerned, had a considerable target smeared on its back as a large number of MasterCard numbers. Programmers are even progressively focusing on private companies since they realize that entrepreneurs will regularly put off actualizing suitable security. There's just no workaround on the off chance that you expect to acknowledge charge card installments other than declining to store that data any more drawn out than you need to.

What it indeed comes down to is the confide in issue. Clients believe you with their charge card data. They think you to be a genuine seller of the items and administrations you give. They think you can make it right if things don't go surprisingly. One could contend that the Blockchain can remove a portion of the cerebral pains from procuring their rehash business.

At the point when it's put away in a way that can't be changed in any capacity, it makes it simpler for all gatherings required to point to what indeed happened, which makes it less demanding to determine any issues.

This is a conspicuous motivation to acknowledge Bitcoin installments. While it likely won't supplant charge cards among clients who think about accommodation, you're exploiting the components of Bitcoin that make it conceivable to acknowledge installments without your clients' close to home data being associated with the exchange. At that point, you can merely log that the payment was gotten without associating their numbers with their names.

The Blockchain can help with the administration of your necessary information when you think about influencing your IT to staff look capable. No one's messages are going to vanish and, regardless of whether an email server has an emergency, the information will even now be recoverable in situations where the hard drive didn't get destroyed. The Blockchain gives decentralization, moment ongoing reinforcements, and an even lower danger of losing your significant information to an equipment disappointment. If losing your considerable information like private messages will prompt any outrage or potentially loss of trust, utilize the Blockchain and ensure all hubs remain up and running however much as could be expected.

A few enterprises need to manage clients who are justifiably anxious about misrepresentation.

Others need to manage directions that represent the treatment of records. At the point when actualized admirably, the utilization of advancements like the Blockchain can console clients and controllers that you're willing to go "well beyond" to verify that records are dealt with appropriately and can't be changed in any capacity once they've been added to the framework.

It may sound irregular that a trustless innovation may help produce trust. Nonetheless, the most critical thing to recollect about the Blockchain is that you don't host to believe the third gathering to try and comprehend what they're doing. You can only ensure you have all your vital information bound on a couple of Blockchain applications and after that merely provide you know some experts around who can guarantee that everything is running efficiently. That way, you won't ever need to stress over things turning out badly because your records got messed with.

All The Best, Darrell Frost

www.ingramcontent.com/pod-product-compliance
Lightning Source LLC
Chambersburg PA
CBHW030048230526
45471CB00003B/996